MW00881301

ST[...]
GOD'S PEOPLE

ROBERT H. HORTON, B.Sc.(Econ.)

Illustrated by Juliette Palmer

Li Tin (2)
F. 1A

EDWARD ARNOLD

© Robert H. Horton 1962

First published 1962
by Edward Arnold (Publishers) Ltd
41 Bedford Square, London WC1B 3DQ

Edward Arnold (Australia) Pty Ltd
80 Waverley Road, Caulfield East
Victoria 3145, Australia

Reprinted 1962, 1963, 1964, 1966, 1968, 1969,
1970, 1972, 1973, 1974, 1975, 1976, 1977,
1978 (twice), 1979, 1980 (twice), 1981 (twice), 1983, 1984, 1985

ISBN: 0 7131 1226 3

The Complete Course comprises:

Book 1: Stories of God's People

Book 2: Stories of Jesus and His Teaching

Book 3: Early Bible Stories and Stories of the Prophets

Book 4: Stories of the Early Church

Book 5: What the Bible is and How it was Written

Book 6: Men who gave us our Faith and our Bible

By the same author:
A Book of Bible Puzzles with Answers
From Abraham to Solomon: 48 Workcards
(*This pack may be used in conjunction with* Book 1
Stories of God's People)
The Life of Jesus: 48 Workcards
(*This pack may be used in conjunction with* Book 2
Stories of Jesus and His Teaching.)
Beginnings and Servants of God: 36 Workcards
(*This pack may be used in conjunction with* Book 3
Early Bible Stories and Stories of the Prophets)
Birth of the Christian Church: 36 Workcards
(*This pack may be used in conjunction with* Book 4
Stories of the Early Church)

Printed in Great Britain by The Bath Press, Avon

PREFACE

THE object of these books is to satisfy a pressing need for a simple and straightforward account of the Bible Story, told in language which can be readily understood by students attending senior classes in Primary education or lower Secondary classes. The author is the teacher responsible for Religious Instruction in a large English Secondary School.

Every effort has been made to keep closely to the original story. The introduction of modern, liberal ideas has been avoided: the inspiration and authority of the Scriptures have been maintained. In the interests of keeping each 'lesson-chapter' reasonably short, it has not always been possible to include every detail of a story. However, this leaves ample scope for the teacher to fill in the details, and for the student to make good use of his Bible.

The importance of the constant use of the Bible in conjunction with the course has been kept in mind. At the end of each chapter suggestions have been included for 'Things to Do'. Many of these involve simple reference to specific Bible passages, and the writing and/or learning of some of them. Naturally, teachers will have many other ideas concerning writing, art, or craft activities.

Illustrations in the course have been kept simple, so that all students should be able to trace or copy without too much difficulty: the artistic will find scope for their ability in the adding of detail and colour. If the suggested activities are carried out, each student should have a collection of Bible texts, illustrations, and useful details, which will be an interesting summary of his year's work.

R. H. H.

CONTENTS

CHAP.		PAGE
1	The Call of Abraham	7
2	Abraham and Lot	9
3	The Birth of Isaac	11
4	The Sacrifice of Isaac	14
5	A Wife for Isaac	16
6	Esau and Jacob	19
7	Jacob's Ladder	21
8	Jacob in Haran	23
9	Jacob comes Home	25
10	Joseph's Dreams	27
11	Joseph goes to Egypt	30
12	Joseph in Prison	32
13	The Pharaoh's Dream	34
14	Joseph, Ruler of Egypt	36
15	Joseph's Brothers come to Egypt	38
16	Joseph's Silver Cup	41
17	Israel in Egypt	44
18	The Birth of Moses	46
19	The Burning Bush	48
20	The Ten Plagues	50
21	Crossing the Red Sea	53
22	Into the Desert	56

Contents

CHAP.   PAGE

23   The Ten Commandments 58

24   Spies are sent to Canaan 60

25   Rahab and the Spies 62

26   Into the Promised Land 65

27   The Battle of Ai 67

28   The Men of Gibeon 69

29   Gideon and the Midianites 71

30   Samson 74

31   Samson and Delilah 77

32   Ruth 79

33   The Boy Samuel 81

34   The People ask for a King 84

35   David anointed King 86

36   David and Goliath 89

37   David and Jonathan 91

38   Saul pursues David 93

39   David the King 96

40   Solomon 98

41   The Two Kingdoms 101

STORIES OF GOD'S PEOPLE

CHAPTER 1
The Call of Abraham

WHEN he was a boy, Abraham lived with his father and mother in the city of Ur. His father was rich, and they lived in one of the many fine houses in the city. The people of the land had strange gods: the Sun, the Moon, and many others. In Ur a great temple was built for the Moon god.

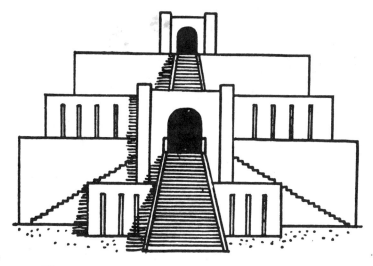

The great temple to the Moon god at Ur may have looked like this.

Abraham's parents used to worship the Moon god, but they began to think that there must be a greater God who had made the sun, the moon, and the stars, and all that was in the earth. When Abraham's mother died, his father left Ur, and took Abraham and Lot, his grandson, far away to the north, to live in the town of Haran.

7

At Haran, Abraham's father died, and Abraham became chief of the tribe. He heard the voice of God calling to him. It was the voice of the God who, Abraham felt sure, was far greater than the Sun god and Moon god of his people.

'Leave your home and your friends,' said God to Abraham, 'and go to a new land which I will show you. There you will be

This map shows how Abraham went from Ur to Haran and Canaan.

the father of a great nation, and I will give you the land to live in.'

So Abraham obeyed the voice of God, and set off for a new land, away in the south. He took with him his wife, Sarah, his nephew, Lot, and all his servants, flocks, and herds, and left Haran to find the 'Promised Land', the land which God had promised to give him.

What a great sight it must have been to see them go. As Abraham was very rich, he had many camels. On some of them rode the women; others carried tents, rugs, and all the other things that they needed. Then there were the donkeys, each with its load to carry. There were the cries of the sheep, the cattle, and the goats, and the shouts of the men who drove them. So they moved slowly away, and left behind them, for ever, the town of Haran which had for many years been their home.

The map (page 8) shows the way that Abraham went from Ur to Haran, and from Haran to the Promised Land. The Promised Land is called Canaan. You can work out how many miles Abraham had to go.

THINGS TO DO

Draw a picture of the temple to the Moon god at Ur. You can make a model of the temple from cardboard or wood.

Write out and learn God's call and promise to Abraham: you will find it in Genesis 12, verses 1-3.

Find out from verse 4 how old Abraham was when he left Haran.

Trace the map on page 8. Show the route Abraham took from Ur to Haran, and from Haran to the Promised Land.

CHAPTER 2

Abraham and Lot

SLOWLY Abraham and Lot, their servants and thousands of animals made their way to the south. Each day they went only a short way, because the flocks had to find food and water, and the young ones could move only at a slow pace. But at last they came into the Promised Land. There were now so many animals that it was hard to find water and grass for all of them. Here and there were wells with stones hollowed out to be filled

9

with water, so that the animals could drink. Sometimes Abraham's men and Lot's men fought to find the best grass and water for their flocks and herds. Often the fight would be near one of the wells.

When Abraham saw what was going on he told Lot that it

Here and there were wells with stones hollowed out to be filled with water, so that the animals could drink.

would be best if they left each other and went different ways. As chief of the tribe Abraham could have the best land if he wanted it, but he was kind and gave Lot the first choice.

'If you go to the right,' Abraham told Lot, 'then I will go to the left; if you go to the left, then I will go to the right.'

Lot looked from the hill where they stood, over all the land that lay in front of him. Below him he saw the flat land near the River Jordan with its green grass, its trees and plenty of water. Around him were the rocky hills with little grass and few streams. Lot said, 'I will go down into the plain and live there, among the villages and cities.'

So Lot took his servants, his flocks and his herds, and went down into the plain leaving Abraham to wander among the hills.

Once again Abraham heard the voice of God speaking to him and saying, 'Look to the north and to the south, to the east and to the west. All the land that you can see is yours. I will give it to you and to your children. It will be yours for ever.'

THINGS TO DO

Draw a picture of a well where the flocks could drink. You can make a model using plasticine or clay.

Abraham was very rich. What did he own? You can find the answer in Genesis 13, verse 2.

Write out the promise made by God to Abraham after Lot had left him. Genesis 13, verses 14-15.

What was the name of the city near which Lot pitched his tent? What does the Bible say about the people of this city? You can find the answers in Genesis 13, verses 12-13.

CHAPTER 3

The Birth of Isaac

As Abraham and Sarah had to move from place to place, they could not live in a proper house. They had to have a home that could be put up and taken down easily, and was not too heavy to carry with them. This home was a tent of cloth made from goat-hair. The cloth was put over three rows of three poles each, and held by cords and tent-pegs. More cloth hung down to make the walls of the tent. The men used one part, the women used another, and between them was a wall, or curtain, of cloth. On the floor were mats and carpets to make

Abraham's home was a tent of cloth made from goat-hair.

the tent more like a home. Water-jars, water-skins, cooking pots, lamps, and a grindstone were to be found in the tent. Some of these things, and the food, could be kept in the low end parts of the tent.

Abraham and Sarah grew older. They were rich and happy, but there was one thing they did not have, a son. How they wished that they had a son. And how could God keep His

Isaac 艾萨克

promise to give the land to Abraham and his children if they had no children? God knew what Abraham was thinking. Once more God spoke to him and said that he would have a son. He told him to go and stand at the door of the tent as night fell.

'Look at the stars,' said God, 'and see if you can count them. You will be the father of many children, as many as the stars that you can see.'

Abraham and Sarah were happy now, and soon a son was born. They called him Isaac, and he grew up to be a fine, strong boy. As he grew older he was able to help with the work about the tents, and to take care of the animals. Abraham taught him all that he knew, and he told him about God. As Abraham watched him at work and at play he knew that, one day, Isaac would follow him as chief of the tribe. So God's promise would come true. But Abraham did not know that very soon God would test his faith by asking him to kill Isaac as a sacrifice to God.

THINGS TO DO

Draw a picture of Abraham's tent. You can make a model of the tent from some dark cloth, cotton, and sticks.

Make a list of some of the things to be found in the tent.

Write out from Genesis 15, verse 5, God's promise to Abraham: the word 'seed' means children or descendants.

Verses 5 and 15 of Genesis 17 tell how Abraham and Sarah were given their names by God. Write these names and their meanings: ABRAHAM = Father of a great multitude; SARAH = Princess.

13

CHAPTER 4

The Sacrifice of Isaac

ONE day God spoke to Abraham again.

'Take your son, Isaac, the son you love so much, and go to a hill that I will show you. There you must make an altar and kill Isaac and burn him as an offering to Me.'

Abraham was very sad at this, but he had great faith in God and he knew that he must obey God's word.

Early the next day Abraham got up, put the saddle on his ass, cut some wood, and called two of his men to go with him and Isaac. For three days they made their way to the place that God had told him about. At last Abraham saw the hill still a long way off. Then he left the two men with the ass and told them that he and Isaac would go up the hill to make a sacrifice to God.

Isaac took up the wood, and Abraham took some fire and his knife. On the way up the hill Isaac said, 'Father, we have the wood and the fire; where is the lamb?'

'God will see that we have a lamb, my son,' said his father.

At the top of the hill Abraham took some stones and made an altar, and laid the wood in its place. He tied Isaac and put him on the wood, and then Isaac knew that he was to take the place of the lamb. Abraham took his knife and held it up, ready to kill his son. Then he heard the voice of God again:

'Stop! Do not harm the boy. You have shown me how great is your faith.'

How glad Abraham was. He untied Isaac, and then, as he turned round, he saw a ram that had its horns stuck fast in a bush. Abraham took the ram, killed it, and burned it as an offering to God in place of his son. How happy they were as they made their way down the hill again.

14

Abraham took his knife and held it up, ready to kill his son.

THINGS TO DO

Draw a picture of the sacrifice of Isaac. You can make a model of this scene, using stones, sticks, and plasticine.

Write out the verse in which God told Abraham what he must do: Genesis 22, verse 2.

What was the name of the land to which Abraham was sent?

Can you think why Abraham took wood with him when he went up the mountain?

What did God say to Abraham when he was about to kill his son? Genesis 22, verse 12.

CHAPTER 5
A Wife for Isaac

THE years went by, and Isaac grew to be a man. Abraham was very old and weak, and he knew that the time had come to find a wife for his son, as was the custom in those days. He wanted Isaac's wife to be one of his own people, from the land that he had left so many years ago. Abraham was too old to go back to Haran, so he chose a servant, a man who had been with him a long time, to go and find a wife for Isaac.

The servant took some of Abraham's camels and set off for the north, perhaps along the same way that Abraham had come when he first left Haran to find the Promised Land. After many days he came to the well near the walls of Haran. It was evening, the time when the women came to the well to get water for their homes. The man sat down not far from the well. What was he going to do? How was he to find a wife for Isaac? He prayed to God, and asked that the first woman to give him a drink and to draw water for his camels should be the right one.

Almost at once he saw a girl coming along the path that led from the town. Her name was Rebekah, and she was very beautiful. The man watched her as she drew up the water and filled her pitcher, then he went up to her and asked her for a drink. Gladly she gave him some water, and said, 'I will draw water for your camels, too.' This she did, until the camels had drunk enough.

Abraham's servant knew then that God had heard his prayer, and that this girl was to be Isaac's wife. He went with her to her home, and told her father and mother why Abraham had sent him to Haran. All of them knew that God must have chosen Rebekah, and that she must go back with the man to Abraham.

The servant gave many gifts to Rebekah and to her parents.

16

Then he set her on one of the camels and led her from Haran to the tents of Abraham. So she came to Isaac who loved her as soon as he saw her, and she became his wife.

He saw a girl coming along the path that led from the town.

THINGS TO DO

Draw a picture of the well where Abraham's servant met Rebekah.

Why was the servant told to choose a wife for Isaac from the town of Haran, so far away? You will find the answer in Genesis 24, verses 2-4.

How many camels did the servant take with him? Genesis 24, verse 10.

What presents did he give to Rebekah? Genesis 24, verse 22.

Copy this 'family tree' of Abraham, Isaac, and Rebekah:

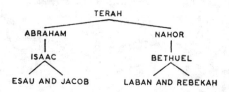

TERAH

ABRAHAM   NAHOR

ISAAC   BETHUEL

ESAU AND JACOB   LABAN AND REBEKAH

From this you can see how Isaac and Rebekah were related.

CROSSWORD: Copy the squares below into your book. Then, in the open squares, fill in the answers to the clues 'Across'. When you have done this you will find the answer to the clue 'Down'.

All the answers can be found in Chapters 1-5 of this book.

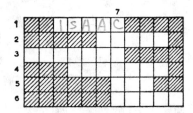

CLUES ACROSS: 1. This son made two old people happy.
2. Once the home of Abraham.
3. He once lived in the city of Ur.
4. A servant met her at a well.
5. This man went to live in the plain.
6. This name means 'Princess'.

CLUE DOWN: 7. Abraham had many of these.

18

CHAPTER 6
Esau and Jacob

ISAAC and Rebekah lived happily together and had twin sons. They were called Esau and Jacob. When they grew up, Esau's skin was rough and hairy; he was a great hunter and loved to

Esau agreed to give Jacob his birthright for a bowl of soup.

be out in the open air. Jacob liked to stay at home among the tents. Their father liked Esau better because he was strong and manly, and because he brought Isaac the meat he loved, the meat of the deer. Rebekah loved Jacob better, as he was always at home with her.

One day Esau had been out hunting. He came home tired out, and found his brother Jacob at the fire making soup. So hungry

was Esau that he agreed to give Jacob his birthright for a bowl
of soup. The birthright was his right to be next chief of the tribe.

Later, when Isaac was very old and nearly blind, he sent
Esau to hunt deer and bring him some meat. After this, Isaac
was going to give Esau his blessing. Rebekah heard what Isaac
said to Esau, and, when he had gone to hunt, she told Jacob to
kill two kids from the goats so that she could cook them for
Isaac. Her plan was for Jacob to take Esau's place, and so to
take his brother's blessing from his father. But first she had to
put the skin of the goats on Jacob's arms and neck, for he had
a smooth skin, not at all like Esau's. His father would not see
him, but he would feel that it was Jacob, and not Esau.

So Jacob went into Isaac's tent and gave him the meat. His
father thought that the voice was Jacob's voice, but, when he
felt his skin, it was the skin of Esau. When he had eaten, Isaac
felt stronger and blessed his son, Jacob, making him the next
chief. Later, Esau came back, and his father found out what
had been done. He could not take back his blessing, and Esau
was very angry. He made up his mind that he must kill his
brother. When Rebekah knew this, she told Jacob that he
must run away.

'Go to my brother, your uncle, in the town of Haran,' she
said, 'and stay there until your brother forgets his anger.'

So Jacob fled from the tents of Isaac, and made his way into
the hills, along the road by which his mother had come, many
years before, to marry Isaac; the road to Haran.

THINGS TO DO

What were the differences between Esau and Jacob? Find
the answer in Genesis 25, verses 25 and 27.

Jacob took two things from Esau. What were they? Genesis
25, verse 33, and Genesis 27, verse 35.

What was the name of the meat of the deer? What weapons
did Esau use. The answers are in Genesis 27, verse 3.

What made Isaac think it was Jacob, and not Esau? Genesis 27, verse 22.

Write out Isaac's blessing for Jacob. Genesis 27, verses 28-29.

CHAPTER 7

Jacob's Ladder

RUNNING away from home and from the anger of his brother, Jacob made his way among the hills. He had a lot to think about: how he had taken Esau's birthright; how he had stolen by a trick his father's blessing. The sun was setting as, tired and hungry, he came to a rocky place where he could rest for the night. He took for his pillow one of the many stones that were about, and lay down to rest.

Then Jacob had a strange dream. In the dream he saw a ladder standing on the earth, and the top of it seemed to go right up to Heaven. On it, going up and down, were angels, and at the top was God Himself. God spoke to Jacob, 'I am the God of Abraham, your grandfather, the God of Isaac, your father. All the land which is around you, I will give to you and to your children. Your family will spread to the west and to the east, to the north and to the south. I will be with you everywhere you go and, one day, I will bring you back to your home again.'

Jacob woke up, full of wonder and fear, saying to himself, 'God is here. This must be the House of God.' Early that morning he took the stone that he had used for a pillow, stood it on end, and made it into an altar to God, pouring on oil from the horn which he had with him. He called the place where he had seen God in his dream Beth-el, which means 'the House of God'.

Before he went on his way Jacob made a vow: 'If God will be with me, and will look after me wherever I go; if He will give me food and clothing, and bring me safely back home; then

He shall be my God, and this stone that I have set up shall be God's house.' So Jacob left Beth-el and set off again, along the road that led to Haran, the town where his mother, Rebekah, had lived as a girl.

Jacob took the stone that he had used for a pillow and made it into an altar to God.

THINGS TO DO

Draw a picture of the place where Jacob had his wonderful dream, or make up a picture of his dream.

Write out Jacob's dream. Genesis 28, verse 12, and the first part of verse 13.

Write down the name that Jacob gave to the place, Genesis 28, verse 19, and then write the meaning of this name, 'House of God'.

Write out Jacob's vow. Genesis 28, verses 20-1.

CHAPTER 8

Jacob in Haran

AFTER many weary days Jacob came near to the town of Haran. He saw a well, with many sheep waiting for the shepherds to give them water. As he watched, another flock of sheep came up, led by the girl who was in charge of them. They were the sheep of Laban, Jacob's uncle and his mother's brother. The girl was Laban's daughter, Rachel, and she was very beautiful. Jacob went to the well and moved away the stone that covered it, then he drew water for Rachel's sheep. When they had all drunk, Jacob went back with the girl to her father's house and stayed there with the family.

Jacob looked after Laban's sheep and cattle, but, although he was like one of the family, Laban would not let him work for nothing. Jacob said that he would work for seven years if, at the end of that time, he could marry Rachel. Laban gladly agreed. The seven years passed quickly for Jacob and the day of the wedding came. A great feast was made ready and the bride came in, her face hidden by a veil. When Jacob was married to her he found out, to his anger and dismay, that he had married Leah, Rachel's elder sister. Laban told him that he could not marry the younger sister until the elder one was married; that was the custom of the land. So Jacob, who had tricked his brother and his father, had now been tricked himself.

But Jacob was not one to give up hope. In those days many men had more than one wife, and Jacob agreed to work for Laban for another seven years so that he could marry Rachel.

23

Once more the seven years passed quickly, and Rachel at last became his wife.

For another six years Jacob stayed with Laban, now working

Jacob moved away the stone and drew water for Rachel's sheep.

so that he could have a share of the flocks and herds. Then he took his wives, his eleven sons and a daughter, and a great number of sheep, and cattle, and goats, and began the journey back to his own home, the home from which he had fled twenty years before.

THINGS TO DO

Draw a picture of the meeting at the well.

What did Jacob say he would do if he could marry Laban's daughter? Genesis 29, verse 18.

Write how Jacob grew rich and say what he owned. Genesis 30, verse 43.

The name of the place where Jacob and Laban parted was Mizpah, meaning 'watch-tower'. Write out the verse, Genesis 31, verse 49.

CHAPTER 9

Jacob comes Home

As Jacob made his way home he began to think about his brother, Esau, and how he had tricked him twenty years before. Would Esau still be angry? Would he still want to kill him? In his fear, Jacob divided his people, his camels, herds and flocks into two bands. If Esau and his men came to fight one band, then the other would be able to escape. He prayed to God, 'You have been good to me; now save me, I pray, from Esau my brother, for I am afraid.'

Then Jacob took some of his animals as a gift for Esau, so that he would forget his anger: two hundred and twenty goats, the same number of sheep, thirty camels and their young ones, forty cows and ten bulls, and thirty asses. He sent his servants forward with them in groups, one after the other. When they met Esau they were to say, 'These belong to your brother Jacob, and they are a present for Esau. Jacob is coming behind us.'

So Jacob sent all his people, flocks and herds, across the stream into his own land again. He stayed behind, alone, to think. And God came to him and said, 'No longer shall your name be Jacob; you shall be called Israel, a prince of God.'

As the sun rose the next morning, Israel—for that was now his name—crossed the stream and saw, coming towards him,

Jacob sent his servants with the animals as a gift for Esau.

his brother Esau and four hundred men. As he came near Israel bowed before him, and Esau ran up and threw his arms around his brother and kissed him.

'What are all these animals that I have seen?' asked Esau.

'They are a gift, my brother, for you,' said Jacob. Esau was already rich in flocks and herds, and did not want more, but Jacob made him take the gift.

Then Jacob went on his way. Another son was born to Rachel, so Israel now had twelve sons. At last he came back to the tents of his father, Isaac, who was still alive, but now very old. How glad Isaac must have been to have his son back after so many years.

THINGS TO DO

Write out the verse which tells of the meeting of Jacob and Esau. Genesis 33, verse 4.

God gave Jacob a new name. Write the verse which tells this, Genesis 35, verse 10. Now write down the meanings of the two names:

JACOB = Supplanter   ISRAEL = Prince of God.

Besides his twelve sons, Jacob had a daughter. What was her name? You will find it in Genesis 34, verse 1.

In Genesis 35, verses 28-29, we read how old Isaac was when he died. How old was he?

CHAPTER 10

Joseph's Dreams

JOSEPH was next to the youngest of Israel's twelve sons. His father was very fond of him because he reminded him of Rachel who had died when the youngest son, Benjamin, was born. He gave Joseph a special coat. It was a coat of different colours, with long sleeves, the kind worn by a ruler rather than by a worker. Perhaps Israel had made up his mind that Joseph would be the next chief instead of his eldest brother. Joseph was very pleased with his coat, but his brothers were angry and jealous.

27

His brothers called Joseph 'the dreamer' because he had so many dreams. In those days people thought that a dream had a meaning—perhaps God was speaking in the dream and saying what He was going to do. Joseph was only young, and

His brothers' sheaves bowed down to Joseph's sheaf.

his brothers were very jealous of his dreams because they seemed to show that he would one day be greater than they.

One day, Joseph told his brothers about one of his dreams.

'We were in the cornfield, making sheaves,' said Joseph, 'when my sheaf stood up, and yours stood round and bowed down to mine.' When they heard this his brothers were very angry. Did the dream mean that Joseph, the dreamer, would rule over them?

28

Joseph's Dreams

Soon after this, Joseph had another dream. This time his father was there when he was telling his brothers.

'In my dream,' said Joseph, 'the sun, the moon and eleven stars all bowed down to me.' Even his father was angry at this, because he saw the meaning of the dream.

'Shall your mother and I and all your brothers bow down to you?' Israel asked.

His father and his brothers did not know then that, one day, these dreams were to come true, and that they would bow down to Joseph.

THINGS TO DO

CROSSWORD : Copy the squares below into your book. Then, in the open squares, fill in the answers to the clues 'Across'. When you have done this you will find the answer to the clue 'Down'.

All the answers can be found in Chapters 6-10 of this book.

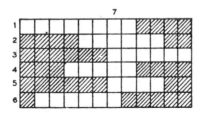

CLUES ACROSS :   1. He was a youngest son.
2. He was a dreamer.
3. A man worked 14 years for her.
4. Rebekah's brother.
5. This man was a hunter.
6. This name means 'House of God'.

CLUE DOWN :   7. This name means 'Prince of God'.

Draw a picture of one of Joseph's dreams. You can make a model of the dream about sheaves of corn, using pieces of straw and cotton.

29

How old was Joseph at this time? Genesis 37, verse 2.

Write out the verse which tells why Israel loved Joseph, and what he gave to Joseph. Genesis 37, verse 3.

Write out the verses which describe Joseph's dreams. Genesis 37, verses 7 and 9.

CHAPTER 11

Joseph goes to Egypt

JOSEPH'S brothers looked after their father's flocks. Often they went a long way to find water and good grass for their animals. They were sometimes away from home for many days, even weeks. One day, when they had been away with the flocks for some time, Israel sent Joseph to see how they were. He put on his coat of many colours and set off to find his brothers.

He had a long way to go, and he had to ask many people if they had seen his brothers, but at last he found them. When they saw him coming, a long way off, one of them said, 'See, here comes the dreamer. Let us kill him, and see what happens to his dreams. We can say that a wild animal has killed him.' But the eldest brother, Reuben, tried to save Joseph from them. Near by was a pit which was used to hold water for the sheep. Just then it was dry. 坑 [pit]

'Let us not kill him,' said Reuben. 'Put him in this pit, while we make up our minds what to do with him.' He hoped that later he could pull Joseph out of the pit and send him home.

So, when Joseph came up to them, his brothers took his coat and put him in the pit. While they sat round it, talking and eating their meal, a caravan of merchants came by on their way to Egypt. Another brother had an idea.

商人 商队 [kærə'væn] 怒火 [mɔːtʃənt] [ai'diə]

'Come on,' he said, 'let us sell Joseph to these merchants as a slave, and then we have no need to kill him.'

So Joseph was sold and when Reuben, who had not been

The pit was probably like this. Joseph could not climb out without help.

there at the time, came to pull him out of the pit, he was too late.

Then the brothers took Joseph's fine coat, killed one of the goats, and dipped the coat in its blood. They took the coat back home to their father. Israel knew it at once.

'This is Joseph's coat,' he said. 'Some wild animal must have killed him.' And Israel wept for his son.

31

THINGS TO DO

Draw the pit into which his brothers put Joseph.

Where did Joseph's brothers take their flocks? Genesis 37, verse 12.

Where did Joseph find his brothers? Genesis 37, verse 17.

Write out the verse which tells about the brothers' plot. Genesis 37, verse 20.

How much was Joseph sold for? Genesis 37, verse 28.

CHAPTER 12
Joseph in Prison

WHEN the merchants who had bought Joseph from his brothers came to Egypt, they sold him to Potiphar. He was an officer of the Pharaoh, King of Egypt. Joseph was now a slave, but God did not forget him. He was a good servant to his master, and after a time he was made head of all the servants. So well did Joseph work that his master did not need to worry at all about the house or the other servants.

However, Joseph displeased Potiphar's wife and she told lies to her husband about him. Her husband believed what she told him and was very angry. He had Joseph put into prison. But even here God was with Joseph, and very soon the jailer gave him the job of looking after the other prisoners.

It was in prison that Joseph met two of the king's servants, the butler and the baker. They had displeased their master in some way. Each of the men had a dream while they were in prison, and when they told Joseph about their dreams he was able to tell them what the dreams meant.

The butler said, 'In my dream I saw a vine with three

branches. I took the grapes and squeezed the juice from them into the king's cup.' 'The three branches are three days,' said Joseph, 'and in three days the king will send for you and make you his butler again.'

'In my dream,' said the baker, 'I had three baskets of cakes

The butler dreamed about grapes, the baker about baskets of cakes.

on my head, and the birds came down and ate the cakes.' 'The three baskets,' said Joseph, 'are three days. In three days the king will send for you and hang you, and the birds will eat your flesh.'

What Joseph had told the two men came true: the butler went back to his job; the baker was hanged. The butler had told Joseph that when he went back to his work he would speak to the king about him so that he could be freed from prison. But once he had left the prison the butler forgot all about Joseph.

THINGS TO DO

Draw a picture of the baker's and the butler's dreams.

Write out the verse which tells what the merchants did with Joseph. Genesis 39, verse 1.

Write the verse which tells how God was with Joseph, even in prison. Genesis 39, verse 21.

What special day was it when the butler's and the baker's dreams came true? Genesis 40, verse 20.

CHAPTER 13

The Pharaoh's Dream

THE butler, whose dream had come true as Joseph had said, went on with his work and forgot Joseph. Then another dream made him think about the man he had met in the prison. This time it was a dream of the Pharaoh, or King of Egypt.

One morning, the king called all his wise men and told them that he had had a strange dream. He told them what he had seen in his dream, but not one of them was able to say what it meant. It was then that the butler remembered his own dream, and the baker's in prison two years before; he remembered, too, that Joseph had told them what their dreams meant. Now he told the king about this, and the king sent for Joseph to come from the prison.

When Joseph came, the king said, 'I have had a dream, and

34

no one can tell me what it means. I hear that you can tell the meaning of dreams.'

'Not I,' said Joseph, 'but God will give you an answer.'

So the king told Joseph about his dream.

'In my dream,' said the king, 'I was standing by the river Nile. Out of the water came seven fat cows, and began to eat the grass on the river <u>bank.</u> Then seven thin cows came up out

Joseph told the king the meaning of his dreams.

of the river, and they ate up the first seven. Yet the thin ones were no fatter, they were still poor and thin, as at first. Then I dreamed again. I saw seven strong, fat ears of corn, all on one stalk. Then I saw seven more, thin and withered, and they ate the first seven. What does this mean?'

'The two dreams are really the same,' said Joseph. 'God has been telling you what He is going to do. The seven cows and the seven ears of corn are seven years. There are going to be seven years of good crops in Egypt, and there will be <u>plenty</u> to eat. After them will come seven years of <u>famine</u>, and the good years will be <u>forgotten</u>, because there will be no crops. This is the meaning of the dream, and this is what God is going to do.'

THINGS TO DO

Draw a picture of the Pharaoh, or a picture of one of his dreams.

How long was Joseph in prison after the butler was set free? Genesis 41, verse 1.

What did Joseph do before he came into the Pharaoh? Genesis 41, verse 14.

Write out Joseph's reply when the Pharaoh asked him to tell the meaning of his dream. Genesis 41, verse 16.

Write out the verses which tell the meaning of the dream. Genesis 41, verses 29-31.

CHAPTER 14

Joseph, Ruler of Egypt

WHEN Joseph had told the Pharaoh what his dream meant, and what God was going to do, he said, 'Now, let the king find a wise man and make him ruler of Egypt. He can <u>choose</u> other men to help him in his work. In each of the seven years of plenty let them take <u>one-fifth</u> of the crops and save it for the bad years that are to come. Then there will be food in the land, and no one will be hungry.'

The king saw that this was a wise plan.

'Can we find anyone better than the man who has told me the meaning of my dream?' asked the king. 'He is wise, and

God is with him. He shall be ruler of all Egypt, under me.'
Then the king gave Joseph his own ring to wear as a <u>sign</u> that
he was ruler, and a gold <u>chain</u> for his <u>neck</u> and fine clothes.
He rode in a <u>chariot</u>, and the people bowed down to him as
he passed.

During the seven years of plenty Joseph put the corn into great store-houses.
(This is how Egyptians drew pictures.)

Joseph was now about thirty years old. Not long before he
had been a <u>slave</u>: now he was a great man, second only to the
king. Perhaps he thought about his life as a boy, at home with
his parents and brothers; and about the dreams that were now
to come true.

During the seven years of plenty Joseph went round the

計算

land of Egypt. He saved so much corn and other food that there was too much to count. It was put away in great store-houses in all the towns of the land.

Then the years of plenty ended and, as the king had seen in his dream, the years of famine began. There were no crops and the people were hungry. They went to Joseph and he opened up the store-houses and sold corn to the people of Egypt. In other lands, too, there was famine, and many people, hearing that there was corn in Egypt, came to Joseph to buy food.

THINGS TO DO

Draw a picture of a grain store in Egypt.

Write out the verse which tells us how the Pharaoh made Joseph ruler of Egypt. Genesis 41, verse 40.

How old was Joseph at this time? Genesis 41, verse 46. How long was this since he first came into Egypt? You can find the answer by looking at your answers to Chapter 10 of this book ('Joseph's Dreams').

Write out the verse which tells how much corn Joseph stored. Genesis 41, verse 49.

Now write a verse which tells us that people of other lands came to Egypt to buy corn. Genesis 41, verse 57.

CHAPTER 15

Joseph's Brothers come to Egypt

WHILE Joseph in Egypt was busy with his great stores of corn, his father (Israel) and his brothers were short of food. There was a famine in Canaan, too.

'I hear that there is corn in Egypt', said Israel to his sons. 'Go and buy some, so that we shall not <u>starve</u>.' *hungry to die* [std-v]

So Joseph's brothers set off for Egypt. The youngest, Benjamin, stayed at home with his father.

After many days the brothers came into Egypt, and at last

His brothers knelt before Joseph, thus making his dream of long ago come true.

they came to Joseph. He knew them at once, but they did not know him. Since they had sold him as a slave he had grown to be a man; he wore <u>Egyptian</u> clothes, and, as an Egyptian, he had no beard. They <u>knelt</u> before Joseph, thus making *Knee* *Kneel* *Knelt* his dream of long ago come true, and told him that there

39

was a famine in their land and they had come to buy corn.

'No!' he said. 'You are spies: you have come to spy in Egypt.'

'We are twelve brothers,' they said. 'The youngest is at home with our father, and another is dead.'

Joseph pretended that he still thought they were spies, and he put them in prison for three days. Then he said, 'I want to see your young brother, to prove that your story is true. One of you must stay in the prison until your brother comes to me.' So one brother, Simeon, was kept in prison, and the others were sent home with the corn that they had come to buy.

On the way home, one of the brothers opened his sack to give his ass some food, and there in the top of the sack was the money that he had paid for the corn. When they came home to their father all the brothers found the same thing—there was the money in the top of their sacks. They told Israel all that had happened in Egypt, what the ruler had said about Benjamin, and how Simeon was in prison.

Israel was very sad, afraid that Benjamin might be lost as Joseph had been lost. The brothers were afraid too. They thought that, somehow, all that had happened to them in Egypt was to do with the way they had treated Joseph.

THINGS TO DO

Draw a picture of Joseph's meeting with his brothers.

Write the verse which tells how Jacob (Israel) sent his sons to Egypt for corn. Genesis 42, verse 2.

How did Joseph's dream come true? Genesis 42, verse 6. You will remember Joseph's dreams in Chapter 10 of this book.

Joseph told his brothers that they were spies. What did they answer? Genesis 42, verse 13. Which two brothers did they mention, and what did they say about them?

What did Jacob say when he was told that Benjamin had to go to Egypt? Genesis 42, verse 38.

CROSSWORD : Copy the squares below into your book. Then, in the open squares, fill in the answers to the clues 'Across'. When you have done this you will find the answer to the clue 'Down'.

All the answers can be found in Chapters 11-15 in this book.

CLUES ACROSS : 1. Joseph was put into this by his brothers.
                2. The King of Egypt.
                3. River of Egypt.
                4. This brother was kept in prison.
                5. He was an Egyptian officer.
                6. The brother who tried to save Joseph.

CLUE DOWN : 7. Joseph spent some time here.

CHAPTER 16

Joseph's Silver Cup

THERE was still famine in the land of Canaan. Israel and his sons had eaten all the corn that they had brought from Egypt. Once more Israel told his sons that they must go to Egypt for corn.

'Unless Benjamin goes with us, the man will not let us have corn,' one of them told him. Israel did not want Benjamin to go, but he had to agree. He gave them presents for the ruler,

41

and twice as much money, so that they could pay back what
they had found in their sacks.

Again they made the long trip to Egypt and stood in front
of Joseph. This time he took them to his own house so that they

The silver cup was found in Benjamin's sack.

could eat with him. They gave him their gifts and then sat
down in the places Joseph gave to them. To their surprise they
were given places in order of their age, and they could not
understand how the ruler knew their ages. When the food was
put in front of them Joseph gave Benjamin five times as much
as any of the others.

Joseph's Silver Cup

Then Joseph told his servants to <u>fill</u> the sacks with corn, to put each man's money in the top of his sack, and to put his own silver cup in Benjamin's sack. All this was done, and the next morning the brothers set off for home. They had not gone far when Joseph sent servants after them saying that one of them had stolen his silver cup. The brothers said, 'If the cup is in any man's sack then he shall die, and the rest of us will be your servants.' When the sacks were opened there was the cup, in Benjamin's sack.

The brothers went back to Joseph in great <u>fear</u>. Joseph said that they could go home, but the one in whose sack the cup had been found must stay as his slave. 'How can we go,' asked Judah, 'and leave our brother? It will break our father's heart. Let me stay in his place and be your slave.'

Joseph could not <u>pretend</u> any more. He saw that his brothers no longer cared only for themselves: they were thinking of their father. The time had come to <u>forgive</u> them for all that they had done to him. He sent his servants out, and when they were alone he said, 'I am Joseph, your brother, <u>whom</u> you sold. Do not be afraid, it was God's will. Now go home and bring our father and your families. I will find a place for you to live in Egypt.'

THINGS TO DO

Draw a picture of Benjamin finding Joseph's cup.

Which brother promised to look after Benjamin. Genesis 43, verse 8.

What did Israel tell his sons to take to the ruler of Egypt? Genesis 43, verses 11-12.

How did Joseph's servant make the brothers welcome? Genesis 43, verse 24.

Write out the two verses which give Joseph's message to his father. Genesis 45, verses 9-10.

CHAPTER 17
Israel in Egypt

WHEN the King of Egypt heard about Joseph's brothers, he told him to send wagons and horses and to bring his father, Israel, to Egypt. Joseph gave his brothers clothes, food and animals,

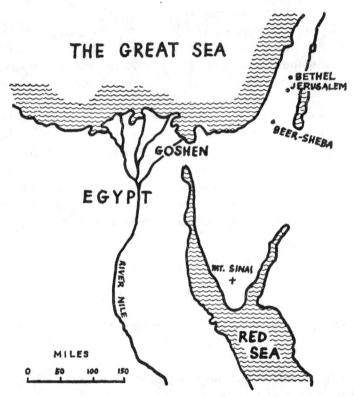

Israel made a sacrifice to God at Beer-sheba before he went to live in the land of Goshen.

and sent them on their way. When his sons told Israel that Joseph was alive and that he was the ruler of Egypt, he could not believe it. But when he saw all the wagons and the many gifts that Joseph had sent, he knew that what his sons said must be true. He agreed to go back with them to Egypt, to meet the son he had lost so many years ago.

So the whole family moved into Egypt: Israel, his sons, their wives, and their children, and all that they had. They were given the land of Goshen to live in. How happy they all were to be together again. For seventeen years Israel lived in the land of Goshen, and then he died, an old, old man. The years went by, and Joseph, too, grew old and died.

All this time the children of Israel, their animals and their crops grew in number, until the land of Goshen was filled with them. Long after the death of Joseph, a new king who had not known him saw how many Hebrews there were, and how their crops and animals had grown.

'See,' he said, 'the Hebrews are stronger than we are; there are too many of them. They may join with our enemies, or even drive us from our own country.'

Something had to be done and the Egyptians made the Hebrews slaves, and set task-masters over them. They were made to build cities and store-houses, to make mortar and bricks, and to do all kinds of hard work in the fields. Still the Hebrews grew in number. Then the Pharaoh did a cruel thing.

'Every girl that is born,' he said, 'you must save alive, but every boy you must throw into the river Nile.'

Many baby boys were thrown into the river, but one boy was saved, a boy who many years later was to save his people from Egypt. His name was Moses, and his story begins in the next chapter.

THINGS TO DO

Draw a map to show where the Children of Israel settled in Egypt.

Write the two verses in which God spoke to Israel and made him a promise. Genesis 46, verses 2-3.

Describe how Joseph went to meet his father. Genesis 46, verse 29.

The Children of Israel grew in number and wealth in Goshen. Write the verse which tells us this. Genesis 47, verse 27.

Write out the verse which tells of the cruel way in which the Pharaoh treated the Israelites. Exodus 1, verse 22.

CHAPTER 18

The Birth of Moses

WHEN Moses was born his mother hid him for three months to save him from the Egyptians. But as he grew older she could not hide him any more. So she made a basket of reeds and coated it with pitch to keep out the water: then she put the baby Moses inside and hid the basket in the rushes at the edge of the river. His sister, Miriam, stayed not far away, to see what would happen to the baby.

Soon the king's daughter came to the river to bathe, and when she saw the basket she sent her maid to fetch it. She opened it, and there was Moses crying. The princess felt sorry for the baby and knew that it must be one of the Hebrew boys. Then Moses' sister came up and said, 'Shall I ask one of the Hebrew women to mind the baby for you?' The princess told her to do this, and Miriam went and asked her own mother to look after Moses. So Moses' mother cared for him until he was old enough to go and live with the princess as her son.

Moses grew up as an Egyptian prince, but in his heart he knew that he was a Hebrew. Perhaps his mother had told him all about himself and his people before she gave him to Pharaoh's daughter.

One day, many years later, when Moses was a man, he went out to watch his own people at work. He saw one of the Egyptian task-masters beating a Hebrew slave. This made him angry and he hit the task-master so hard that he killed him. Then he was afraid, but, as no one seemed to have seen, he dug a hole in the sand and hid the body.

46

The next day, as he went out, he saw two Hebrew men fighting. He asked one, 'Why are you hitting your friend?'

The basket was hidden in the rushes at the edge of the river.

'Are you going to kill me as you killed the Egyptian yesterday?' the man said. 僻遠的 秘密的

Then Moses knew that what he had done was no <u>secret</u>. [ˈsiːkrɪt] The king would be angry and would try to kill him. What must he do? He must run away. So Moses fled from Egypt and went to the land of Midian.

47

THINGS TO DO

Draw a picture of the basket among the reeds. You may put in the Pharaoh's daughter and her maids.

Write the verse which tells what Moses' mother did when she could no longer hide her baby. Exodus 2, verse 3.

There are two verses which tell how the Pharaoh's daughter found Moses. Write them out. Exodus 2, verses 5-6.

The Pharaoh's daughter gave the baby the name, Moses, see Exodus 2, verse 10. Write down the name and its meaning:

MOSES = Drawn out (of the water).

When the Pharaoh heard what Moses had done to one of the task-masters, he was angry. Write the verse which tells of this. Exodus 2, verse 15.

CHAPTER 19
The Burning Bush

WHEN Moses came into the land of Midian he sat down to rest by a well. Seven girls, daughters of the priest of Midian, came to the well for water for their father's sheep. When they had drawn the water some shepherds came along to drive them away, so that they could use the water first. But Moses helped the girls who went home and told their father that an Egyptian had helped them. The priest told them to bring Moses back with them so that he could take food and drink. Moses stayed with the priest, became his shepherd, and married one of his daughters.

One day, when Moses was out with the flocks, he saw a strange sight. It was a bush which seemed to be on fire but did not burn away. He went nearer to see what it was, and then he heard a voice speaking to him. It was the voice of God saying, 'Do not come any nearer. Take off your shoes, you are on holy ground.'

Then God went on, 'I have seen how badly the Egyptians treat my people, and I will save them from Egypt. I will bring

When Moses threw his rod on the ground it turned into a snake.

them back to the Promised Land. You must go to the Pharaoh and bring my people out.' Moses was afraid: he did not want to go back to Egypt, so he began to make excuses. How could he prove that God had sent him?

'Throw your rod on the ground,' said God, and when Moses did this it turned into a snake.

49

'Now,' said God, 'take it by the tail.' Moses did so, and it was a rod again.

Then Moses said, 'I cannot go to the Pharaoh, I do not speak well, I am slow at speaking.' God was angry with Moses.

'Aaron, your brother, speaks well: he will speak for you.'

So Moses went back to Egypt and met his brother, Aaron, and told him how God had spoken to him from the burning bush. Then the two men spoke to the leaders of the Children of Israel (the Hebrews), and told them what God had said, and how they must bring the people out of Egypt.

THINGS TO DO

Draw a picture of the burning bush.

What was the name of the priest of Midian? Exodus 3, verse 1.

Moses married his daughter. Find her name in Exodus 2, verse 21, and write it down in your book.

Write out the verse which tells of the strange sight that Moses saw. Exodus 3, verse 2.

When Moses came near to the bush, God spoke to him. What did God say? Exodus 3, verse 5.

What did God want Moses to do? Write out Exodus 3, verse 10.

CHAPTER 20

The Ten Plagues

WHEN Moses and Aaron came to the Pharaoh and asked him to let their people go to worship God in the desert, he would not agree. He did not want to lose his slaves. He even made

50

them work harder. They had been given <u>straw</u> to make the <u>clay</u>
bricks stronger, but now the king said, 'Let them go and <u>gather</u>
straw for themselves, but still they must make as many bricks
as before.'

Moses told the king that <u>disasters</u> would come to Egypt if he

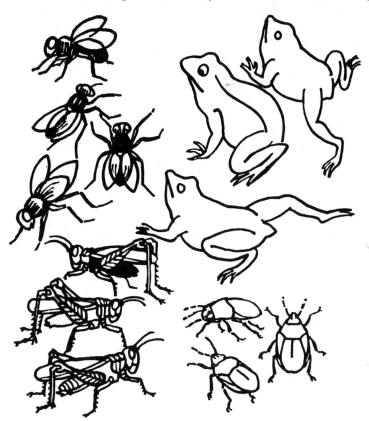

Among the plagues were frogs, flies, lice and locusts.

did not let the people go. Still he would not agree, and God sent
ten <u>plagues</u> to make him change his mind. First of all the river
Nile became red and <u>smelly</u>, so that the water was not <u>fit</u> for
the people to drink. Then great numbers of frogs came up from
the river into all the streets and houses. After this came a plague
of <u>lice</u>, <u>tiny</u> insects which <u>swarmed</u> on the people and the

51

animals. Each time a plague came the king said that he would let the people go, but as soon as the plague had gone he changed his mind and would not let them go.

Next came a great swarm of flies; then the animals grew sick and many of them died. After this came <u>boils</u>, on people and animals <u>alike</u>. Thunder and lightning and <u>hail</u> <u>spoiled</u> the crops. Then, from the east, the wind brought a great swarm of <u>locusts</u> into the land of Egypt, and they ate up all that was green in the land, all the grass, and the leaves of <u>bushes</u> and trees. After this came <u>darkness</u>, so that no one could see: the air was filled with sand and <u>dust</u>. But even then the king would not let Moses take his people away.

The last plague was <u>worse</u> than all the others. During the night the first-born child of every Egyptian family died, and the first-born of every animal. Only the Hebrews were safe. This was too much for the Egyptians, and that same night the king sent for Moses.

'Go from among my people,' he said, 'and <u>worship</u> God as you want.' So Moses led the people out of Egypt into the desert, and they made their way towards the Red Sea.

THINGS TO DO

Draw a picture to show what some of the ten plagues may have been like.

Write out the verse which gives God's promise to the Children of Israel. Exodus 6, verse 7.

After each plague the Pharaoh promised to let the people go. Write the verse which tells how he changed his mind. Exodus 8, verse 32.

Write out the tenth and last plague. Exodus 12, verse 29.

What did the Pharaoh say to Moses that night? You will find his words in Exodus 12, verses 31-32.

How many people did Moses lead out of Egypt? Exodus 12, verse 37.

CROSSWORD: Copy the squares below into your book. Then, in the open squares, fill in the answers to the clues 'Across'. When you have done this you will find the answer to the clue 'Down'.

All the answers can be found in Chapters 16-20 of this book.

CLUES ACROSS: 1. The Hebrews were this in Egypt.
2. Joseph sent these to fetch his father.
3. Found in Benjamin's sack.
4. There were ten of these.
5. The part of Egypt where the Hebrews lived.
6. The Hebrews had to make this for the Egyptians.
7. He was found among the rushes.

CLUE DOWN: 8. Sent by God to plague the Egyptians.

CHAPTER 21

Crossing the Red Sea

MOSES wanted his people to get away from Egypt as quickly as possible. He did not lead them straight to the Promised Land, but south towards the mount of God, Mount Sinai. He knew this part of the land well, for it was there that God had spoken to him from the burning bush.

But when the Hebrews had left, Pharaoh was sorry that he had let them go. He had lost his slaves.

God spoke to Moses: 'Hold out your rod over the sea.'

'Why have we done this? Why have we let the Hebrews go?' he said.

He took six hundred chariots and many horsemen and soldiers, and went after the Hebrews to bring them back. The Hebrews were moving slowly, and it was not long before the army of the Pharaoh came in sight of them. As they looked back the Hebrews were afraid. They could see a long way off a cloud of <u>dust</u>: they knew that it must be the Egyptians coming after them. There was no <u>escape</u>. The Red Sea was in front of them, the Egyptians were behind.

The water in front of them was not the Red Sea itself, but one of the <u>shallow</u> lakes to the north. It was called the Reed Sea, or Sea of Reeds, and this was where the Children of Israel were to go across the water. God spoke to Moses, '<u>Hold out</u> <u>your rod over the sea, and my people will go across safely</u>.' So Moses held out his rod. The east wind drove back the shallow water until the people were able to go on in safety. The great crowd passed slowly across the sea. The first of them <u>reached</u> the other side, and soon the whole crowd of people were safely across.

They turned to watch the army of the king of Egypt follow them into the waters of the sea. But the wind had now dropped and the water began to <u>flow</u> back and to get deeper again. Soon the wheels of the Egyptian chariots were <u>stuck</u> fast in the wet sand. Horses and men, in great fear, tried to turn back. But it was too late. The water flowed over them until not an Egyptian was left. At last the Children of Israel were safe from their enemies.

THINGS TO DO

Draw a picture of Moses and the Children of Israel at the Red Sea.

When the Israelites saw the Egyptian army coming after them, they were afraid. Write out what Moses said. Exodus 14, verses 13-14.

What did God tell Moses to do? Exodus 14, verse 16.

Two verses tell us how the Children of Israel crossed the Red Sea. Write them out. Exodus 14, verses 21-22.

Now write the verse which tells how God destroyed the Egyptians. Exodus 14, verse 28.

CHAPTER 22

Into the Desert

FROM the Red Sea Moses led his people to the south, towards Mount Sinai. It was desert, and soon the people were thirsty and hungry. How glad they were to see, far off, the waters of

The dotted line shows the way that the Children of Israel went when they left Egypt.

Marah. But when they got there the water was bitter and not fit to drink. Moses took the branch of a tree and threw it into the water, and the water became sweet. Then on they went to Elim, where there were twelve wells and seventy palm trees. Here they made their camp with plenty to eat and drink.

From Elim their way led through the desert once more.

56

Again they had no food or water. But God did not forget them. In the morning there lay on the ground a mass of small, white, sweet things. 'Manna,' said the people, using a word which means, 'What is this?' Each morning they went out to gather the manna, enough to feed them all. And at night they had meat to eat. A great flock of quails flew over and came down to land near the Children of Israel. The quail is a fat, heavy bird like a partridge, and it cannot fly far at a time. These birds were tired out, and it was easy for the people to catch them.

Water was still the great need of the Children of Israel. At Rephidim, Moses found some limestone rock which often holds water. He took his rod and struck the rock with it. Out ran a stream of water for the people to drink.

It was near here that the Children of Israel were attacked by the men of the tribe of Amalek. Moses was too old to fight, and Joshua led his people. Moses stood on the hill with his arms held up in prayer to God. While the people could see his arms up they knew that God was with them and they began to win the fight. But when Moses dropped his arms because they were tired the people lost heart, and the men of Amalek began to win. Aaron and Hur stood by Moses and held up his tired arms, and as the sun went down the men of Amalek were beaten and fled.

THINGS TO DO

Draw a map to show the journey of the Israelites through the wilderness.

Write two verses which tell how God fed His People. Exodus 16, verses 14-15. Make a note of the name of the food and its meaning: MANNA = 'What is it?'

God gave them water, too. Write out this verse. Exodus 17, verse 6.

What did Moses tell Joshua to do, when the tribe of Amalek came? Exodus 17, verse 9.

CHAPTER 23

The Ten Commandments

ABOUT three months after they had left Egypt, the Children of Israel came to Mount Sinai. They made their camp at the foot of the mountain. Moses told the people that this was the mountain of God, and that no one must go up. But he himself went up the mountain to speak with God. It was there that God gave him ten laws for the people. These were the Ten Commandments. The first four were about the duty of the people to God: they must have no other gods, nor make any idols, they must not use God's name in the wrong way, and they must keep God's day holy. The other laws were about their duty to other people: they must honour their parents; they must not kill; they must be faithful to one another; they must not steal; or tell lies; or long for things that were not theirs.

Moses came down the mountain with these laws on two tablets of stone. When he came near to the camp he heard singing and shouting, and he wondered what it meant. He had been away many days, and the people did not know what had become of him. They thought that he was not coming back. So they had asked Aaron to make them an idol to worship. Aaron knew that this was wrong, but he wanted to please the people. He asked them to give him their golden rings and ear-rings, and from them he made a great, golden calf. The people danced and sang round the calf, and it was this noise that Moses heard.

How angry Moses was when he saw what was going on. He threw down the tablets of stone in his anger, and broke them in bits. He took the calf and broke it up, and told the people that they must never do such a thing again. Then he had to go back up the mountain to write out again the laws that God had given to him.

A wooden box was made to hold the Ten Commandments. This box was called the Ark. It was carried on poles by

58

the priests, and it was the sign of God's presence with His people.

The Tabernacle and the Ark.

So that they would have a place where they could worship God, Moses had a special tent made. It was called the Tabernacle. Wherever they went this tent was put up as a church, with the Ark inside to show that God was there.

THINGS TO DO

Draw a picture of the Tabernacle and the Ark.

Copy out this short form of the Ten Commandments:

(You will find the Ten Commandments in the first 17 verses of Exodus 20.)

1 Thou shalt have no other gods.
2 Thou shalt not make any image.
3 Thou shalt not take God's Name in vain.
4 Remember the Sabbath day.
5 Honour thy father and mother.
6 Thou shalt not kill.
7 Thou shalt not commit adultery.
8 Thou shalt not steal.
9 Thou shalt not bear false witness.
10 Thou shalt not covet.

Write out the verse which tells what Moses did when he saw the golden calf. Exodus 32, verse 19.

CHAPTER 24
Spies are sent to Canaan

As the Children of Israel made their way to the north, Moses sent out twelve spies, one for each of the twelve tribes of Israel. The tribes were named after the twelve sons of Israel. They went out in pairs into the land of Canaan, to see what the land was like, and to find the best way of winning the country. The map in Chapter 22 shows from where the spies went to Canaan.

When they came back they brought with them the fruits that they had found: grapes, figs, peaches, olives; they brought many other kinds of food too.

'It is a land flowing with milk and honey,' the spies said.

They meant that there was plenty to eat and drink in Canaan.

'But the cities are strong and have great walls, and the people are giants,' the spies went on. Only two of them, Joshua and Caleb, said that the Children of Israel must go in and take the land at once. The people were glad to see the fruits that the

60

spies had brought back, but they were afraid to go on. They did not listen to Joshua and Caleb, but thought about what the other spies had said. Many of them said that it would be better to have a new leader who would take them back to Egypt. At least they did not have to fight in Egypt.

From Mount Nebo, God showed Moses the Promised Land.

God was angry with His people. He had led them to this land, and now they were afraid to go in.

'They shall not see the land that I have promised them,' God said; 'they shall die in the desert. The people who came from Egypt shall not enter Canaan.' So the Children of Israel had to wander in the desert for forty years. During those years the older people died and the young ones grew up. The time came

61

for God to lead them back to Canaan. They came to Mount
Nebo near the Promised Land. (See map in Chapter 22.)
Moses went up the mountain and <u>from the top</u> God showed
him the Promised Land. On Mount Nebo Moses died. He had
brought the people safely from Egypt, through forty years in
the desert. Now his job was done. The task of leading them
across the river Jordan into Canaan was not for Moses: it was
for the new leader God had chosen, Joshua.

THINGS TO DO

Draw a map to show how the spies were sent into the
Promised Land. Put in the name of the mountain where Moses
looked over the land. Deuteronomy 34, verse 1—Mount Nebo.
You will be able to add other places to the map as you read
later chapters.

How did the spies describe the land, the cities, and the
people? Write out these verses. Numbers 13, verses 27-28.

What did Caleb say should be done? Numbers 13, verse 30.

CHAPTER 25

Rahab and the Spies

WHEN Moses was dead, God spoke to Joshua.
'Be strong and brave,' He said, 'for I will be with you. I will
give you and your people this land to live in.' But before
Joshua took the people into the Promised Land he sent out two
men to spy on Jericho, the city just across the river Jordan.
The two men stayed in the house of a woman named Rahab.
Like many other houses, this one was built on the city wall.
The king of Jericho heard that there were spies in his city, and
he sent soldiers to Rahab to make her give them up. But she

hid the men in the flax which was drying on the flat roof of her
house.

The soldiers thought that the spies must have gone back
across the river. They went after them, and the city gates were
closed. Then Rahab brought out the two men and said to

Rahab let the men down from her window.

them, 'I have heard how your God brought you out of the land
of Egypt and across the Red Sea. Now all the people of Jericho
and of the rest of the land are afraid of you, because they know
that God is on your side. Since I have been kind to you,
promise me that when you take this city you will save me and
my family.' The two men gladly made the promise.

Then Rahab told them not to go back to the river at once, but to hide in the hills until the soldiers stopped looking for them near the river. As the city gates were locked, Rahab took a red cord and let the two men down from her window, which was on the outside of the city wall. Before they went they said, 'When our people come across the river, bring all your family here. Tie this red cord in the window so that we shall know the house, and you will all be safe.'

The spies went away and, as Rahab had told them, hid in the hills for three days, until the soldiers had stopped looking for them. When all was quiet they went back across the river Jordan. They told Joshua all that had happened, and how the people were afraid of the Children of Israel because God was with them.

THINGS TO DO

Draw a picture of the city of Jericho.

God spoke some wonderful words to Joshua. Write out the first seven words in Joshua 1, verse 6, and the first seven words in Joshua 1, verse 7.

What was the report of the spies to Joshua? Write out this verse. Joshua 2, verse 24.

CROSSWORD: Copy the squares below into your book. Then, in the open squares, fill in the answers to the clues 'Across'. When you have done this you will find the answer to the clue 'Down'.

All the answers can be found in Chapters 21-25 of this book.

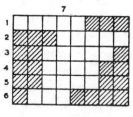

CLUES ACROSS: 1. The Mount of God.

2. There was bitter water here.

3. He went to spy with Joshua.

4. There were twelve wells here.

5. The end of Moses' journey.

6. This held the Ten Commandments.

CLUE DOWN: 7. The tribe conquered by the Israelites.

CHAPTER 26

Into the Promised Land

WHEN Joshua had heard what the two spies had to say, he told the Children of Israel to move down to the river Jordan and be ready to go across. The priests were to carry the Ark into the water first, and show the people the way to go.

The priests carrying the Ark came to the river and stepped into the water. At once a strange thing happened. The river seemed to stop flowing. The priests with the Ark stood still, and all the people were able to go across safely, just as many years before they had gone across the Reed Sea. Twelve men, one from each tribe, took a stone from the river bed. These were set up in a pile, to remind the people of the day that God led them into the land of Canaan.

When all the people had gone across, the priests carried the Ark out of the water, and at once the river began to flow as before. The Children of Israel went on until they came near to the city of Jericho. The city gates were shut for fear of the Israelites.

Then the soldiers of Israel marched round the city, followed by the Ark and the priests blowing on their trumpets. The rest of the people came behind. Each day, for six days, the Children of Israel walked like this round the city and then went back to their camp. But on the seventh day they went round the city seven times. And Joshua said, 'When the priests blow on their trumpets you must all shout aloud, for God has given you the city.'

So, when the people had walked round the seventh time the

The priests carrying the Ark stepped into the river.

priests blew their trumpets, and the Children of Israel gave a great shout. The walls of the city fell down flat, and the city was taken. Only Rahab and her family were saved, as the spies had promised her.

THINGS TO DO

Draw a picture of the priests carrying the Ark across the river Jordan or round the city of Jericho. The picture in the last chapter will help you to draw Jericho.

Write out God's promise to Joshua about Jericho. Joshua 6, verse 2.

Now write out the verse which tells us how the city of Jericho fell. Joshua 6, verse 20.

CHAPTER 27

The Battle of Ai

AFTER Jericho the next city to be taken was Ai. Once more Joshua sent men to spy on the city. They came back and said that it was only a small city, and a small army could take it. Joshua sent about three thousand men. But the men of Ai were able to beat them, and the Children of Israel lost heart. Had God forgotten them? Was He angry with them? But God spoke to Joshua again:

'Do not be afraid. Take all your fighting men and go to Ai. I will give you the city.'

This time Joshua took great care. He chose thirty thousand men and sent them away at night. They hid in the hills to the north of the city. Other men hid to the west of the city. Then, early in the morning, Joshua led the rest of the people towards the gates of Ai. The king of Ai took his men out to meet them, not knowing that there were many of Joshua's soldiers hidden near the city.

As the men of Ai came near to Joshua, the Children of Israel pretended to be afraid. They ran away, chased by the men of Ai. The gates of the city were left open, and not a man was left in Ai. Then Joshua stopped. He held up his spear in the air. This was a sign to his hidden soldiers. Quickly they came out, ran into the city, and set it on fire. Joshua and his soldiers turned round to face the enemy. The men of Ai were trapped. In front of them was the great army of Israel. Behind them, as they looked, they saw the smoke rising into the air from the fire that was burning down their city. They lost heart, and soon they were beaten, and their city was destroyed.

Joshua called all the people together. He read to them the words of the laws that Moses had given them. Then he made an altar to God to thank Him for His help in taking the city of Ai.

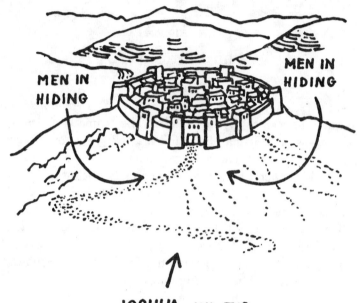

JOSHUA AND THE ISRAELITES

This picture shows Joshua's plan to capture Ai.

THINGS TO DO

Draw a sketch to show Joshua's plan to capture the city of Ai.

Put Ai and Jericho on the map that you drew for Chapter 24.

Write out the three verses which tell how Ai was captured. Joshua 8, verses 15, 16, 19.

CHAPTER 28

The Men of Gibeon

THE news of the fall of Jericho and Ai made the people of Canaan afraid of the Children of Israel. The city of Gibeon was

'Our clothes have become old and worn with the long journey.'

very near to Ai, and its people tried to think how they could escape. Some of their men were sent to Joshua to make peace with him. They had a clever plan to make Joshua think that they had come from a far-off land.

They put on old, torn, dusty clothes; their shoes were old and mended; their wine-skins were torn and dirty; their bread was dry and mouldy. They looked as if they had come many,

69

many miles. When Joshua saw them he asked them who they were.

'We have come from a far land,' they said. 'We have heard about your God, how He brought you out of Egypt, and how He has led you here. So we have come to make peace with you. Our clothes and our shoes have become old and <u>worn</u> with the long journey; our bread was hot from the oven when we left; and our wine-skins were new.'

Joshua thought that the story told by the men was true. He made peace with them. Then, three days later he found that they were from the city of Gibeon only a few miles away. The Children of Israel were very angry. Many of them thought that these men, who had told them lies, ought to be put to death.

But Joshua said, 'No! We have made peace with them, we cannot kill them. We will punish them by giving the men of Gibeon <u>humble</u> work to do for us. They shall draw water and cut wood for us.' These were the most humble jobs that the people had to do.

After this, the Children of Israel went through the land taking many towns and winning many <u>battles</u>, until they <u>spread</u> over all the land of Canaan.

THINGS TO DO

Draw a picture of the meeting of Joshua and the men of Gibeon.

Put Gibeon on the map you have drawn.

Make a list of the things done by the men of Gibeon to make Joshua think that they had come a long way. Joshua 9, verses 4-5.

Now write out what the men of Gibeon said. Joshua 9, verses 12-13.

How did Joshua punish the men of Gibeon? Write out the first 13 words of Joshua 9, verse 27.

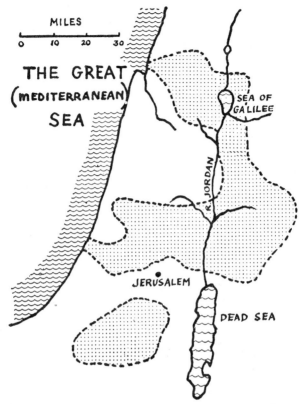

The dotted parts of the map show where the Children of Israel first settled in Canaan.

CHAPTER 29

Gideon and the Midianites

THE Children of Israel <u>settled</u> in the land of Canaan. Often they were not united, but were divided into twelve tribes. Only in times of great danger or war did they join together under leaders who were called judges. Gideon was one of these judges.

The Midianites had beaten the Children of Israel, who often had to hide in caves in the hills. Their enemies stole their crops

71

and made the Children of Israel very sad. Where was the God who had brought them here? But God did not forget them.

One day God spoke to Gideon:

'I will be with you, and you shall save my people from the Midianites.' Gideon called together the men of Israel and a great army was gathered. But God told him that he had far too

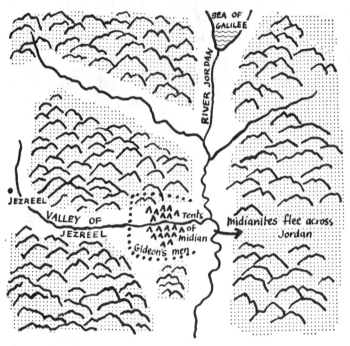

The black dots show how Gideon's men surrounded the camp of Midian.

many men. He must send home any who were afraid. Many of the men went home, but still God said that there were too many.

'Take them to the stream to drink,' said God. Gideon did this, and many of the men threw themselves down by the water to drink. But three hundred of them took up the water with their hands, so that they would be ready and on guard for any attack of the enemy.

72

'By these three hundred I will save Israel,' God said. 'Send the rest away.'

Gideon gave to each of his three hundred men a trumpet, a pitcher and a torch hidden in the pitcher. At night they took their places round the camp of the Midianites. Then, at the sound of Gideon's trumpet each man broke his pitcher, held up his torch and shouted aloud. The Midianites were afraid. They thought that they were being attacked by three hundred armies, not just three hundred men. They fled to the river Jordan, where other Israelites were waiting for them. Many of the men of Midian died, and the rest fled to their homes. Once again God had given victory to Israel. His three hundred men had defeated the great army of the Midianites.

THINGS TO DO

Draw a sketch-map to show how the men with Gideon surrounded the Midianites.

What was Gideon doing when the angel of God spoke to him? Judges 6, verse 11.

Write out the words spoken by the angel to Gideon. Judges 6, verse 12.

How many men left Gideon to go home, and how many were left? Judges 7, verse 3.

How did Gideon divide his men? Write this verse. Judges 7, verse 16.

Write out the verse which gives Gideon's orders to his men. Judges 7, verse 18.

CHAPTER 30

Samson

WE have read how the Children of Israel were led by the Judges, men like Gideon, in time of danger. There are many stories about one of these judges, a man called Samson.

The Philistines, who lived in Canaan near the shores of the Great Sea, were fine soldiers. They often beat the Children of Israel and made them their slaves. At one such time a baby boy was born called Samson. God told his father and mother that when he grew up he would save his people from the Philistines.

As a sign that Samson was to be God's man, his parents made a vow that his hair would never be cut, and that he would never shave. When Samson grew up he was very strong. Because of the vow made by his parents, it was said that his great strength lay in his hair. Most of the stories about Samson are about his strength.

One day, Samson was going to one of the Philistine cities. On the way he met a lion in his path. It roared at him as he came up. Samson had no weapon with him, but he took the lion with his bare hands and killed it.

Samson often did things to displease the Philistines. One day he set fire to their fields of corn and vines and olive trees. When the Philistines came to punish him he used his great strength to kill many of them.

After this the Philistines sent a great army to take Samson.

The Children of Israel did not want to fight. Why should they fight because Samson had displeased the Philistines? Samson told them that they could tie him up and hand him over to the enemy. They did this, but when the Philistines came, Samson broke his cords as if they had been cotton. He looked for something to fight with and found a big, old bone on the ground. With the bone he killed so many Philistines that the rest fled in fear.

Later, Samson went to a Philistine city. When they knew

that he was there, the Philistines locked the gates of the city. They thought that their enemy was in their hands and could not escape. But they had forgotten Samson's great strength. He came to the city gates and lifted them from their hinges.

Samson took away the gates and posts of the city.

Then he took the gate posts as well. He took the gates and posts to the top of a near-by hill. Once again the strength that God had given him had helped him to escape from his enemies.

THINGS TO DO

Draw a picture of Samson taking away the gates of the city.

Write out the verse which tells us about the birth of Samson. Judges 13, verse 24.

What had happened to the lion that Samson killed, when he came back to it? Judges 14, verse 8.

How did Samson set fire to the Philistines' corn, vineyards and olives? Judges 15, verses 4-5.

What weapon did Samson use to fight the Philistines, and how many did he kill with it? Judges 15, verse 15.

Write out the verse which tells how long Samson was a judge. Judges 15, verse 20.

CROSSWORD: Copy the squares below into your book. Then, in the open squares, fill in the answers to the clues 'Across'. When you have done this you will find the answer to the clue 'Down'.
All the answers can be found in Chapters 26-30 of this book.

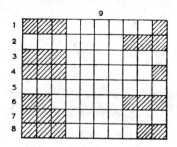

CLUES ACROSS: 1. He followed Moses as leader of the Children of Israel (Israelites).
2. They carried the Ark.
3. The first city to fall to the Israelites.
4. How many tribes were there?
5. These people were conquered by Gideon.
6. Gideon was this.

7. Each of Gideon's men had one of these.
8. She was saved when her city was taken.

CLUE DOWN: 9. Samson was famous for this.

CHAPTER 31

Samson and Delilah

SAMSON married a Philistine woman called Delilah. The rulers of the Philistines asked her to help them to capture their enemy. They said to her, 'Find out the secret of Samson's great strength, so that we can tie him up and punish him for what he has done to us.' They promised her money if she would help. So Delilah said to Samson, 'Tell me the secret of your great strength, and how you can be tied.' Samson said that if he were tied with seven new bow strings he would be weak as any other man. Delilah tied him, and then she shouted, 'The Philistines are here.' Samson broke the bow strings as if they were cotton.

Again Delilah asked Samson to tell her why he was so strong, and how he could be made weak.

'Tie me with new ropes that have never been used, and I shall be weak,' he said. Once more Delilah did this.

'The Philistines are here,' she shouted. And Samson broke the ropes as he had the bow strings before. Each time Delilah tried to find out his secret Samson told her lies.

Day after day Delilah wept and tried to make Samson tell her what she wanted to know. At last Samson grew tired of this and told her the truth.

'If my hair is cut, then I shall be weak,' he said. Delilah knew that this time he had told her the truth. She told the Philistines to come. They brought a man to cut Samson's hair while he was asleep. Then again she shouted, 'The Philistines are here.' Samson awoke and fought with his enemies, but his strength was gone and he was captured.

77

The Philistines took Samson and put out his eyes. They put him in prison, where his work was to grind corn. From time to time they took him into the temple of their god to amuse the

Samson pulled the pillars with all his might.

people. As time went on Samson's hair began to grow again. His old strength began to come back.

One day, Samson was taken to the temple as usual to amuse the Philistines. He spoke to the boy who led him:

'Let me lean on the pillars of the temple.' When he felt the pillars with his hands he prayed to God for strength. Then he pulled the pillars with all his might. They gave way, and the roof fell in. All those who were in the temple and on the roof were killed. Samson himself died, but God had given him strength at the end to destroy his enemies.

THINGS TO DO

Draw a picture of Samson pulling down the pillars of the temple.

What did Samson say was the secret of his great strength? Judges 16, verse 17.

How many Philistines were on the roof of the temple when it fell? Judges 16, verse 27.

In Judges 16, verse 23, you will find the name of the Philistine god. Write his name down.

Write out the three verses which tell how Samson destroyed the temple of the Philistines. Judges 16, verses 28-30.

CHAPTER 32
Ruth

THE story of Ruth, like those of Gideon and Samson, belongs to the days of the Judges. There was a famine in the land. A woman named Naomi (*Nay-o-my*), her husband and their two sons left their home in Bethlehem to live in another land across the Dead Sea. After some years the man died. The two sons married women of the land where they had gone to live. Soon the two sons died too.

After some time Naomi heard that the famine was over in her own land. She wanted to go back home again. She told her daughters-in-law that they must stay with their own people.

They went with Naomi part of the way, and then one of them
went back. But Ruth knew that Naomi had no one to care for
her. She said, 'No! I will stay with you. Where you go I will go.
Your people shall be my people, and your God shall be my

Ruth gathered the corn left by the reapers.

God.' When Naomi saw that Ruth had made up her mind to
go with her, she no longer tried to stop her. So the two women
went to Bethlehem together.

In Bethlehem there lived a man called Boaz (*Bo-as*). He was
rich and had much land, and he was a relation of Naomi's dead
husband. In order to find food, Ruth went into the fields to
gather up the corn that was left by the reapers. She found

herself in the fields of Boaz. When Boaz saw her there he asked his workers who she was. They told him her story, and he was very sorry for her. He was told how kind Ruth had been to Naomi, and how she had come with her to care for her. So Boaz was kind to Ruth. He told his reapers to let Ruth gather corn in his fields. He even told them to drop some corn so that she could gather it more easily. Then he said to Ruth, 'Do not go to work in any other fields. Stay in my fields with the men and women who work for me.'

So Ruth and Naomi had plenty to eat with the wheat and the barley that she gathered in the fields of Boaz. Boaz also gave her barley to take home to Naomi.

Before long Boaz married Ruth. They had a son who was later to be the grandfather of the great king David. So the story that had begun so sadly for Ruth and Naomi ended happily.

THINGS TO DO

Draw a picture of Ruth gleaning in the cornfield.

One of the sons of Naomi married Ruth. What was the name of the girl whom the other son married? Ruth 1, verse 4.

Write down the wonderful words that Ruth said, when she would not let Naomi go back home alone. Ruth 1, verses 16-17.

Boaz was kind to Ruth. Write down the words said by Boaz to his men which show his kindness to Ruth. Ruth 2, verses 15-16.

CHAPTER 33

The Boy Samuel

SAMUEL was one of the great leaders of the Children of Israel. He was a judge, a prophet and a priest, all in one. The prophets were men chosen by God to speak to His people and to teach them about Him. The priests were men who looked after the House of God, which was called the Temple.

Samuel's mother was called Hannah. She had no children before Samuel was born. She was very sad about this and went to the Temple to pray. She asked God to give her a son.

'*Here I am: you called me.*'

'If you give me a son,' she said, 'then I will give him back to you, to serve you.'

The old priest, Eli, saw her lips moving, but he did not hear what she said. He came up and spoke to her:

'May God give you what you ask of Him!' Then Hannah and her husband went back home. In time a son was born.

He was named Samuel, which means 'Asked of God'. When he was old enough Hannah took him to Eli and, as she had promised, she left him with the old priest. Samuel was to help Eli and to serve God in the Temple.

Eli was very old and nearly blind. One night, as Samuel was lying down to sleep, he heard a voice calling his name. He ran to Eli and said, 'Here I am: you called me.'

'I did not call,' said Eli. 'Go and lie down again.' Then Samuel heard the voice again, calling his name. Once more he ran to Eli, but Eli told him that he had not called him. A third time Samuel heard his name. He was sure that Eli was calling. When he went to the old man again, Eli knew that it must be God calling Samuel.

'Go and lie down,' said Eli, 'and if you hear the voice again, say, "Speak, Lord; your servant is listening." ' So Samuel went and lay down again.

Then God spoke: 'Samuel, Samuel.' And Samuel said, 'Speak, Lord; your servant is listening.' God told Samuel that Eli's sons, who were evil men, were not to be the next priests of God. God had chosen Samuel to be His servant. The next day Samuel told Eli all that God had told him.

Samuel grew up to be a prophet. By him God spoke to His people. When Eli died, Samuel was the next priest of Israel and leader of the people.

THINGS TO DO

Draw a picture of the boy Samuel in the Temple.

What was the vow that Hannah made in the Temple? First Book of Samuel, Chapter 1, verse 11.

What did the old priest, Eli, say to Hannah? I Samuel 1, verse 17.

How did Hannah keep her word? Write out the two verses which tell us this. I Samuel 1, verses 27-28.

God called to Samuel four times. What words did Samuel answer the fourth time? Write out the verse. I Samuel 3, verse 10.

Write 9 words which show that God was with Samuel. You will find them in I Samuel 3, verse 19.

CHAPTER 34

The People ask for a King

WHEN Samuel grew old, his sons, like the sons of Eli, were not good men. They were not fit to rule over Israel after him. The Children of Israel came to Samuel as their judge.

'Give us a king to rule over us,' they said. There were kings in other lands, and the Children of Israel wanted to be like other people. Samuel was very angry. The people should have no other king but God. But God spoke to Samuel: 'The people do not want me to rule over them any longer. Give them what they want. But tell them what kind of king he will be.'

Then God told Samuel the man who was to be king.

'A young man of the tribe of Benjamin will come to you,' said God. 'He is to be king over Israel.' The next day a young man named Saul of the tribe of Benjamin was out looking for some asses that he had lost. He could not find them, and at last he came to Samuel. Samuel was a prophet—perhaps he could tell Saul where his asses were. Samuel told him not to look any more, as the asses had gone back home. Then, before he sent him away, Samuel told Saul that he was to rule over Israel, and he anointed him with oil to show that God had chosen him to be king.

Samuel called all the people together to choose their king. They came in their tribes from all parts of the land. Samuel spoke to them:

'If you have a king to rule over you, this is what he will do.

He will take the men for his army, and the women to work in his palaces. He will take the best of your fields and your vineyards. He will take part of all your crops and your animals. You will all have to work for him. And then you will be sorry

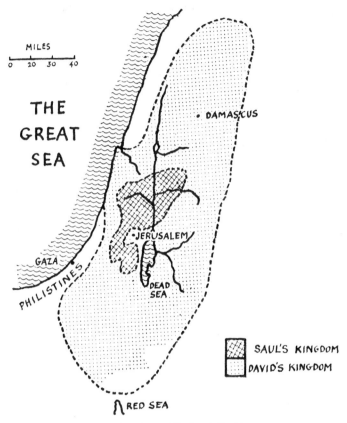

The kingdoms of Saul and David.

that you asked for a king.' But the people would not listen to Samuel.

'We will have a king to rule over us,' they said.

So Samuel chose one tribe, the tribe of Benjamin. From them he took one family, and from the family, one man. This man was Saul. He was a fine man to look at, a head taller than any other man. Samuel brought him in front of the people.

85

'Here is your king,' he said, 'the king God has chosen for you.' And all the people shouted, 'God save the king!'

Saul was a great soldier, but he was not a good king. He led his army to fight the many enemies of Israel. The Philistines were the greatest enemy, and Saul had to fight them all the time that he was king.

THINGS TO DO

Draw a map to show the land which was ruled by King Saul.

In the First Book of Samuel 8, verses 11-17, Samuel tells the people what the king will be like. Make a list of the things that the king would do.

What was the name of Saul's father? I Samuel 9, verse 3.

Write out the verse which tells how Samuel showed the people their first king. I Samuel 10, verse 24.

CHAPTER 35
David anointed King

WHEN Saul was king he did things which made God angry. God spoke to Samuel:

'Saul does not keep my laws. I will not have him as king any more. Go to Bethlehem, to the house of Jesse. I have found a new king among his sons.' So Samuel put oil in his horn, and set off for Bethlehem. He came to the house of Jesse.

Jesse called his sons to stand, one by one, in front of Samuel. The eldest son came first, a tall, strong man.

'This must be the one God has chosen as king,' thought Samuel. But God said to him, 'Do not look at his face or at his size. He will not do. You judge a man by his looks, but I look at his heart.' One by one, the sons came in. Each son was strong and tall. Each time Samuel thought that he had found the right man. So seven of Jesse's sons came to Samuel. But God did not choose any of the seven.

'Are these all your sons?' said Samuel. 'There is still the youngest,' said Jesse. 'He is out looking after the sheep.'

David played for Saul on his harp.

Samuel told Jesse to send for him, so that he could see him too. Before long the youngest son came in. His name was David. He was a fine looking boy, and God said, 'This is the one. Anoint him! He is the next king.'

Samuel took his horn of oil and anointed David to be king, in front of his father and all his brothers. But the time had not

87

yet come for David to begin to rule his people. He went back to his flock and there, looking after his sheep, he learned how to look after God's people.

Saul himself had become ill in mind. From time to time he was sulky and had a bad temper. His servants wanted to find a man who could play well on the harp, so that he could play for Saul when he was ill. One of them said, 'David, the son of Jesse, plays well. He is a fine boy, and God is with him.' So Saul sent for David and David came to live with Saul. When Saul was ill, David played for him on the harp, and Saul was better.

THINGS TO DO

Draw a picture of David playing on his harp for Saul.

Write the verse which tells how God rejected Saul as king and sent Samuel to find a new king. I Samuel 16, verse 1.

There is a verse which tells how God chooses a man. Write out this verse. I Samuel 16, verse 7.

You will find the names of Jesse's three eldest sons in I Samuel 16, verses 6, 8, and 9. Write down their names.

In I Samuel 16, the first part of verse 13 tells how David was anointed to be king, and how God was with him. Write out this part of the verse.

CROSSWORD: Copy the squares on page 89 into your book. Then, in the open squares, fill in the answers to the clues 'Across'. When you have done this you will find the answer to the clue 'Down'.
All the answers can be found in Chapters 31-35 of this book.

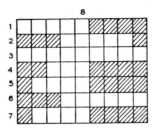

David and Goliath

CLUES ACROSS: 1. He played on the harp.

2. His son was to be a king.

3. A priest went to this city to find a king.

4. An old priest.

5. The first King of Israel.

6. As a young boy he worked in the Temple.

7. She worked in the fields of Boaz.

CLUE DOWN: 8. She gave Samson a lot of trouble.

CHAPTER 36

David and Goliath

THE army of the Philistines, the chief enemy of Israel, was facing the army of Saul. Each army was camped on a hill, and between them was a valley. Each day, the Philistine champion, a huge man named Goliath, came and shouted to the Israelites: 'Send out a man to fight me. If he kills me we will be your servants; but if I kill him, then you shall be our servants.' When they heard this, Saul and his men were very much afraid.

David's three eldest brothers were in Saul's army. One day, their father sent David to them with food. When he reached the army camp he heard the shouts of Goliath and asked what it all meant. David saw that the men of Israel were afraid and he went to Saul.

'I will go and fight with this Philistine,' said David. 'When

I was looking after my father's sheep, a lion and a bear came and took one of the lambs. I went after them and killed them. This Philistine I will kill too, because he has defied God's army.'

Saul gave David his own armour to put on, but it was too

David chose five smooth stones from the brook.

heavy and David took it off. Then he took his staff and went down the hill to the brook. He chose five smooth stones, put them in his shepherd's bag, and took his sling in his hand. He went on to meet the Philistine.

When Goliath saw David he said, 'Am I a dog that you come to me with a stick? Come here to me, and I will give your flesh to the birds.' But David was not afraid of Goliath.

'You come to me with a sword and a spear and a shield,' David said; 'I come in the name of God, and He will give me victory.'

So Goliath came on, and David ran to meet him. As he ran, he took a stone from his bag and put it in his sling. He threw it and hit the huge Philistine on the forehead. Down he fell to the ground. David ran to him, drew Goliath's sword, and killed him. When the Philistines saw that their hero was dead, they fled. The men of Israel followed them back to their own country and defeated them.

THINGS TO DO

Draw a picture of David and Goliath.

Write out the words that Goliath shouted to the army of Israel. I Samuel 17, verse 10.

David was not afraid because he trusted in God. Write out the verse which tells us this. I Samuel 17, verse 37.

Now write the brave words that David spoke to Goliath as he went to meet him. I Samuel 17, verses 45-46.

CHAPTER 37

David and Jonathan

AFTER David had killed Goliath, Saul took him home to live with him. Saul's son, Jonathan, and David became great friends. But, because David was so popular with the people, Saul grew jealous of him. He even tried to kill him.

One day, David was playing his harp in front of Saul. In his hand Saul held a javelin. All at once he threw the javelin at David trying to kill him, but David escaped. Again Saul tried to get rid of him. This time he promised David that he could marry Michal, Saul's daughter, if he went out and killed one hundred Philistines. He hoped that the Philistines would kill David and he would be rid of him. But David did what Saul asked, and Saul knew that God was with David.

Saul even asked his own son, Jonathan, and his servants to

Jonathan took his bow and arrows to the place where David was hiding.

kill David. His great <u>fear</u> was that David and not Jonathan would be the next king. So often did Saul try to kill David, that David fled from him. But he and Jonathan were still great friends, and they made a plan so that David would know if it were safe to go back to Saul.

Jonathan was to take his bow and arrows and to go with his

servant boy to the place where David was hiding. Then he was to <u>shoot</u> three arrows. When the boy went to <u>fetch</u> them, Jonathan would shout to him. If he said, 'The arrows are this side of you,' then David would know that it was safe to come back. But if he said, 'The arrows are <u>beyond</u> you,' then David must go away.

When Jonathan tried to make his father forget his <u>hatred</u> for David, Saul would not listen to him. In his anger he even tried to kill Jonathan with his javelin. So Jonathan went out to David's hiding-place. He shot his three arrows, and then shouted to the boy as he looked for them, 'The arrows are beyond you.' David knew that he must go away. Then the two friends met for what might be the last time.

THINGS TO DO

Draw a picture of the two great friends, David and Jonathan.

Saul was jealous of David. Write the verse which tells how Saul tried to kill David. I Samuel 19, verse 10.

David and Jonathan were great friends. Write the verses which tell us this. I Samuel 18, verses 3-4.

Write the verse which tells how David and Jonathan parted. I Samuel 20, verse 42.

CHAPTER 38

Saul pursues David

WHEN David fled from Saul, he hid in a cave in the hills. His brothers and many of his friends came to join him there. Saul came to look for David and killed many of those who had helped him in any way. Then, for a time, David was safe, because Saul had to go back to fight the Philistines. But when

the battle was over his search for David began again. David was
more at home in the hills, where he had spent so much time as
a boy looking after his sheep. Time and time again he escaped
from the king.

One night Saul lay down to rest in a cave. It was the very

They took the spear and the water-jar from where Saul lay.

cave in which David and his men were hiding. This was David's
great chance to kill Saul, but he would not do it. He cut a
piece from the king's robe while he slept, then in the morning
when Saul had gone, David shouted after him. 'See, here is a
piece of your robe, which I cut off while you slept. My men
wanted me to kill you, but I would not harm the one God has

chosen to be king.' Saul saw that David had spared his life, and he went back home. But David stayed in hiding because he did not <u>trust</u> the king.

Later Saul again came out with his men to find David and to kill him. David was in the hills and saw where Saul made his camp. That night David and one of his men made their way into the camp, and found where Saul lay asleep. His spear was stuck in the ground near his pillow.

'Let me kill him with the spear,' said David's man. But David said, 'No! Take his spear and his water jar, and let us go.' So they took the spear and the water jar from where Saul lay and quietly left the camp.

When they had gone some way, David shouted out to Saul and showed him his spear and water. Saul saw that once again David had spared his life, and he made a promise.

'Come back, David,' said the king, 'and I will not try to harm you any more.' And Saul went back home, but David stayed in the hills. Still he did not trust the word of the king.

Not long after this, the Philistines came again to fight against Israel. When the battle was over both Saul and his son, Jonathan, were dead. The time had come for David to be king. At first he ruled only over the tribes in the south. But soon the tribes in the north asked him to be their king too. So David became the second king of Israel.

THINGS TO DO

Draw a picture to show how David spared the life of Saul.

What was the name of the cave where David hid? I Samuel 22, verse 1.

How many men did David have with him? I Samuel 23, verse 13.

I Samuel 24, verse 10, shows why David spared Saul's life. Write out these words of David.

Who went with David into Saul's camp? I Samuel 26, verse 7.

When Saul and Jonathan were killed in a battle with the Philistines, David was very sad. What did he say about them? II Samuel 1, verse 23.

CHAPTER 39
David the King

When David was made king, he began to make war against his enemies, so that Israel could be at peace. He beat the Philistines and many other enemies, and then marched on Jerusalem. The city was built on a hill, and it was so strong that no one thought that David could capture it. The men of the city were so sure that they shouted to David, 'Even the blind and the lame can defend our city.'

But David knew that there was a tunnel which led from the city to a spring of water on the side of the hill. He found the tunnel and sent some men up into the city. Before the men of the city knew what was happening, the city gates were open and David's men had taken the city. Soon Jerusalem was made David's capital, and the Ark of the Lord was brought to the city.

Not long after this, one of David's sons, Absalom, wanted to be king in his father's place. He had so many soldiers that David had to flee from the city. But in time David gathered his armies and went to fight against Absalom. Although his son had done wrong, David did not want him to be harmed. He gave orders to his men that Absalom should be saved alive.

On the day of the battle, Absalom was riding his mule through a wood. As he rode under a great oak tree his hair was caught in one of the branches, and he was left hanging there. When David's captain heard of this, he went quickly to the place and, although he knew the king's orders, he killed the young man as he hung there helpless.

Full of sorrow for his son, David went back to Jerusalem, to take his place as king once more. Now God gave David peace.

David's men found the tunnel which led to the city.

His enemies had been beaten, and David made his country strong. He was growing old, and had ruled his land for forty years. Before he died, he chose the man who was to be king after him. It was to be another of his sons, Solomon.

THINGS TO DO

Draw a picture of David's men capturing Jerusalem.

Write out the verse which tells us how David became king. II Samuel 5, verse 3.

Where was David made king? II Samuel 5, verse 3.

How old was David at the time? II Samuel 5, verse 4.

How long did David reign altogether? II Samuel 5, verse 4.

How long was he king in Jerusalem? II Samuel 5, verse 5.

Write out the verse which tells how Absalom, David's son, was caught in a tree. II Samuel 18, verse 9.

In II Samuel 22, verses 50 and 51 tell us how David thanked God for helping him as king. Write out these verses.

CHAPTER 40

Solomon

BEFORE he died David told his son, Solomon, that he must build a Temple for God in Jerusalem, a place where the Ark of the Lord could be kept. He even helped Solomon by collecting much of the gold, silver, brass, iron and wood that he would need. It took Solomon many years to build the Temple with its altar and great pillars, its porches and royal palace. Then the Ark was brought with the two tablets of the Commandments which God had given to Moses.

One night, Solomon had a dream. God spoke to him and told him to ask for anything he wanted from God.

'You have made me king, after my father, David,' said Solomon. 'Now, give me wisdom to rule your people.' God was pleased with this answer, and said to Solomon, 'Because you have not asked for riches, or long life, or power, I will give you wisdom: and I will also give you riches and honour. There will never be another king like you.'

It was not long before Solomon's wisdom was put to the test. Two women had each a baby son. During the night one of the babies died, and its mother changed the dead child for the one that was still alive. Next morning, the other woman found the dead baby in her arms, and she knew that he was not her son.

After Solomon died the kingdom was split into two, Israel in the north and Judah in the south.

Each mother said that the living boy was her son, and they brought him to Solomon. When the king had heard the two women, he said, 'Bring me a sword. Cut the boy in two, and each mother shall have a half.'

The first mother, the real mother of the boy, could not let this happen.

'No, my lord,' she said to the king, 'do not kill him. Give him to this other woman.' The second woman said, 'No! Cut him in two. Let each of us have half.'

Then Solomon knew which was the mother of the living boy.

'Do not kill him,' he said, 'give him to the first woman, for she is his mother.' And all the people saw how wise their king was.

But in some ways Solomon was not wise. He made his people work too hard, and took too many taxes from them. When he died, many of the tribes would not have his son as their king. So the kingdom was split into two: ten tribes in the northern kingdom, and two tribes in the southern kingdom. (See the map on page 99).

THINGS TO DO

Draw a map to show the kingdoms of David and Solomon.

When did Solomon have his dream, and what did God say to him? I Kings 3, verse 5. Write out this verse.

Write the verse which tells us what Solomon asked for. I Kings 3, verse 9.

God was pleased with what Solomon had said, and He gave him things that he had not asked for. What were these things? Write out I Kings 3, verses 12-13.

How long did Solomon reign? I Kings 11, verse 42.

Solomon's son ruled over Judah, the southern kingdom. What was the name of this son? I Kings 11, verse 43.

What was the name of the man who was made king over Israel, the northern kingdom? I Kings 12, verse 20.

Solomon

CROSSWORD: Copy the squares below into your book. Then, in the open squares, fill in the answers to the clues 'Across'. When you have done this you will find the answer to the clue 'Down'.

All the answers can be found in Chapters 36-40 of this book.

CLUES ACROSS: 1. A big Philistine.
2. Saul tried to kill David with this.
3. One of David's sons.
4. David took this from Saul while he was asleep.
5. David made this city his capital.
6. David killed one.

CLUE DOWN: 7. This was built by Solomon.

CHAPTER 41

The Two Kingdoms

In the last chapter we read how the kingdom of Solomon was split into two after his death. The northern part was called Israel and the southern part Judah. For more than two hundred years there were two kingdoms, each with its own king. They lay in the midst of other, much bigger lands. Find the names of these lands on the map as we read about them.

Israel soon became weak as it was often at war with Syria. At last, about seven hundred years before Jesus was born, the great empire of Assyria conquered Israel and many of its people were taken away as captives. This was the end of the kingdom of Israel. But for a time Judah was able to hold out against its enemies.

Then Assyria was conquered by Babylon. The empire of Babylon began to grow and at last its armies conquered Judah. Jerusalem and its Temple were destroyed and many Jews were taken away into exile. The exile lasted for about sixty years, until Babylon was conquered by the Persians. Then the Jews

The great kingdoms round about Israel and Judah.

who had been in exile were allowed to go home to their own land. Many of them did so and began to rebuild the Temple and the city of Jerusalem.

The Persians, in their turn, were conquered by the Greeks. For a time this did not affect the Jews and their religion very much. But one Greek king tried to stamp out the Jewish religion. This was too much for the Jews and they rose up in revolt. They even won back their freedom for a time.

Then, about sixty years before Jesus was born, the Romans made Palestine a part of the Roman Empire. They were still its rulers when Jesus was born. The Romans allowed the Jews to carry on with their own customs and to worship their own God. But this was not to last. The Jews hated the Romans and, after many years, they rebelled. About forty years after the death of Jesus the Romans destroyed Jerusalem and the Temple.

We shall be able to read some stories about the two kingdoms of Israel and Judah when we come to Book III. Many of these stories are about the prophets, men chosen by God to teach His people.

THINGS TO DO

Trace the map into your book and put in the names of the great countries which lay around the two kingdoms of Israel and Judah.

Copy this time-chart into your book. (We cannot be sure of some of the early dates.)

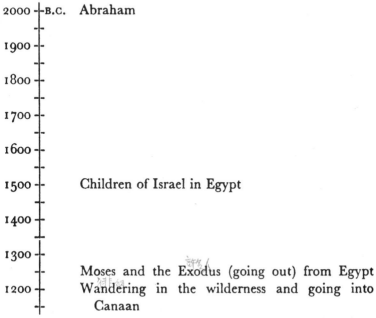

```
2000 ──B.C.  Abraham

1900 ──

1800 ──

1700 ──

1600 ──

1500 ──      Children of Israel in Egypt

1400 ──

1300 ──
                Moses and the Exodus (going out) from Egypt
1200 ──      Wandering in the wilderness and going into
                Canaan
```

103

1100	Time of the Judges
1000	The first kings: Saul, David, Solomon.
	Division of the Kingdom into two 937 B.C.
900	
800	
700	Israel conquered by Assyria 722 B.C.
600	Judah conquered by Babylon 597 B.C.
	The Exile in Babylon 597-537 B.C.
500	Persians allow Jews to return from exile 537 B.C.
	Rebuilding of the Temple
400	Rebuilding of Jerusalem
300	Greeks conquer the Persians 333 B.C.
200	
	Jews revolt against Greeks and win freedom
	160 B.C.
100 B.C.	
	Palestine becomes a Roman province 63 B.C.
0	JESUS OF NAZARETH
	Romans destroy Jerusalem and the Temple 70 A.D.
100 A.D.	